Ronie,

Wishing you
abundant blessings
as you create
your fondest dreams!

Much love,

Aiza

ALIZA McCRACKEN

# CREATIVE ABUNDANCE

## *Artful Possibilities*

*Grace*
PUBLISHING GROUP

CREATIVE ABUNDANCE
First Edition
ISBN 0-9667291-3-7

Designed and Produced by
Aliza McCracken Contemporary Art
Published and Distributed by
Grace Publishing Group in the
United States of America

Printed in China

Companion Art Books
by Aliza McCracken:

*Pure Grace*
*Spirit of Joy*
*The Dance of Love*

www.alizamccracken.com

*Grace*
PUBLISHING GROUP

P.O. Box 42653
Bakersfield, CA 93384
USA

$\mathcal{L}$ive
Joyously,
Creatively,
Abundantly.

# Art Angels

*There are angels among us*
*who bless our hearts*
*and illuminate our paths,*
*inviting us to soar*
*a little higher.*

*You have made a beautiful*
*difference in my life,*
*and for this I am grateful.*
*Thank you for your faithful support.*

*May you be richly blessed!*

The Bakersfield Californian
Banana Republic
Chatté Latté
Robin Coleman & Keely Acebedo
El Adobe
Four Seasons Biltmore
Frugatti's
Nicholas M. Gaona
Gap
Garcia Roofing
The Hornback Family
Daniel D. McCracken
Old Navy
Palace Press International
Paragon Salon & Spa
Pascucci
Pier 1 Imports
Royal Bakery & Cafe
Ruby Sky
Saks Fifth Avenue
Santa Barbara News-Press
Seaward Inn
Target Stores
Sarah Tarmidi
Trader Joe's
Uricchio's Trattoria

# A Bouquet Of Thanks

Creating this art book has been a pure joy, allowing me to express what is true and everlasting.

I give thanks for this divine appointment to be a loving presence to those closest to me, as well as to those in the farthest reaches of the world.

I know there is no separation between us that the love of God cannot embrace.

Out of the abundance of my heart, I am humbly thankful:

To the Creator of this glorious universe, abounded with wondrous delight. Thank you for nourishing the garden of my soul where your endless love, inspiration and guidance sustains me.

To my Family of Angels: for your wonderful gift of prayer support. You are lovely examples of God's creative power and glory.

To Ann Cook, my Design Partner Extraordinaire: for your sacred friendship, abundant goodness and creative harmony.

My heartfelt appreciation to: Marina Picasso, Steven Spielberg, Oprah Winfrey, Ginger Moorhouse, Laura Knight, Julie Hornback, Katherine Abercrombie, Irma Jurkowitz, Leatrice Luria, Marilyn Gevirtz, Lady Leslie Ridley-Tree, Ralph and Anne Fruguglietti, Leni Fé Bland, Oscar Esmaili, Carol Wood, Victor Lopez, Claire Porter, Nick Uricchio, Dr. Randall Schulze, Kelly Pinkham and Philip Morisky for enriching my life in numerous ways. You are remarkable.

My deepest thanks to: all the amazing souls with whom I have the privilege of sharing my dreams.

I adore you profoundly!

# Creative Abundance

My heart is overflowing with love and gratitude for your beautiful letters. I always enjoy hearing from my friends and loved ones. You are beyond amazing!

As you can imagine, I thankfully receive many letters each day. With the volume of requests, it occasionally takes awhile to respond. Yet I sincerely appreciate your wonderful spirit and patience. I pray this art book will nourish your innermost possibilities.

Every soul is of irreplaceable beauty. As God's beloved, we are uniquely designed for a brilliant purpose and plan. We are expressions of divine creativity, worthy of all the honor bestowed upon masterpieces, for indeed we are. In celebrating this expression of life, I wish you abundant blessings as you create your highest dreams.

I joyfully devote this creation to you: in honor of your faithfulness throughout the seasons. Everyday, you remind me of God's splendor in my life and in the world. You so beautifully demonstrate love in its purest form. And I am deeply touched by your affection.

Thank you so much for gracing my path with your magnificent presence and care. May the light of hope shine in your heart now and forever. I love and treasure you all!

Delightfully yours,

$\mathcal{L}$et us be *faithful*
to the calling of
our *hearts*.

$\mathcal{P}$rayer
is at the heart of creativity.
When we *pray*
in faith, all creation moves.

$L$ove is
the most *powerful* force
in the Universe.

$L$ove is

the Divine spark

that ignites

our *creative* passions.

$L$oving faithfully,

opens the door

to an *artful* heart.

*I*n the Spirit of Creativity,

all *dreams* are considered

worthy of love and *respect*.

Make a covenant to living

your highest *vision* using

your *gifts* and resources

to fulfill your dream.

*dream*

*Loving* your *dream* opens

many doors to creativity.

When you shine *unconditional*

*love* on your dream,

the creative process

becomes a *magical* journey.

You can express yourself in more

*tender* and *compassionate* ways.

*love*

*tender*

*L*ove makes the *heart*

a place where *angels* live.

$\mathcal{T}$here is *grace* in every *artistic* endeavor.

Nurture your creativity
with infinite *possibilities*.
As you expand your
*attitude* of mind, you reawaken
to the beauty of your *connection*
with a Higher source.
By *listening* to your true voice,
you will receive greater peace,
*inspiration* and *grace*.

Creating *art* is an act of *faith*.

*A*ll creation flows

from a *limitless*

Divine source.

We can graciously

tap into this source

for the *abundant*

blessings we receive.

The more loving kindness we *share*

the more we *feel* alive, integrated
and *whole*

*E*veryone has the *potential*

for magnificence.

We need to gently release

those blocks that obscure

the pathway to

our *magnificent* selves.

*O*ur creative *essence* is

*timeless* and indefinable.

When we look beyond appearances,

we will discover the essence

of who we truly are...

a loving, *joyful* being who is

*magnificent* beyond compare.

*B*eauty is one of *God's* most valuable treasures.

*B*eauty reflects our *dignity*.

*B*eauty uplifts, *inspires* and guides.

*B*eauty nurtures our inner *possibilities*.

beauty          compassion

reverence        harmony

To behold the beauty of the Lord

is to become a loving beauty

in our hearts and lives.

We can create a more *beautiful* world just by being in it.

When we express *love*,

patience, or forgiveness,

our Spirit grows brighter

and *shines* like a beacon

into the Universe.

*generous*

Be *generous*,

with your Spirit,

for as you do, your capacity

to receive will *overflow*.

We reap the Gifts of Spirit

when we dedicate our lives to

something bigger than ourselves –

the cultivation of *harmonious*

relationships,

a path of service in our community, or

the creation of *beauty* through art.

*K*now that you are

a *beloved* child of God,

and all your dreams

are a natural *expression*

of your divinity.

love

wisdom

creativity

intuition

kindness

forgiveness

surrender

*E*mbrace all the *good*

in the Universe.

Release everything that

no longer serves

your journey.

Let go of all disharmony

and nourish your

fondest *dreams*.

Courage is the *hallmark*

of creativity.

*courage*

Trust in the *creative* process

and let God handle the *details*.

*The* **world** *is our* *playground.*

*P*lay is the doorway to *joy*, innocence and *appreciation*.

*There* are times

when we don't *know*

all the answers. *understand*

When we don't *understand*

*peace* we can *trust*

the One who does.

*experience*

*I*n silence we *experience*

*perfection* the *peace* of

Divine *perfection*.

*L*et go and *surrender.*

Allow the Spirit of Creativity

to *flow* through you

*surrender*

and manifest your dream.

Relax, breathe, and *trust*

that loving guidance is available.

serenity

inner peace

*contentment*

*faith*

*F*aith gives us a door of *hope* to a sweeter, more *abundant* life.

*L*ife on earth is

precious and brief.

If you have

paintings to *create*,

books to write,

songs to sing, and

people to *adore*,

now is the time.

*L*et us *celebrate* life

for the miracle that it is.

Rejoice and give thanks

for the *miracles* of being alive,

being creative, being healthy,

and being loved.

*Live* to your highest awareness

by counting all the miracles

in your *life*.

# May you

*create* a

lifetime of

*beautiful*

*moments.*

# Aliza McCracken

Aliza McCracken is one of those people you feel immediately drawn to – a rare soul with the true ability, despite her busy schedule, to make one feel special and important. Words like "humility" and "grace," terms that normally sound old-fashioned, fit perfectly for this sprite-like beauty.

A Vietnamese orphan, who was adopted into an American family, Aliza feels those experiences have made her a more loving and compassionate person. They have also, she says, shaped who she has become as an artist and spiritual being. A child prodigy, she began painting at age 4, and was an acknowledged professional by the time she was 15. Now at 36, the list of her accomplishments reads like the resume of someone far older.

Photo by Greg Iger

Called a "contemporary artist," the term doesn't even begin to describe her ethereal yet grounded style that soars even as it speaks deeply to our hearts. She has won art awards in Canada, England, Sweden, and the United States, been featured in a growing number of publications, and exhibited her work around the world. Audrey Harrison of ARTscene calls her art "resplendent!" Michael Schumacher, Figaro Contemporary Art, says "She expresses the inexpressible," and Rebecca Allmaras of Eliane Galleries declares that "Aliza paints with the purity of an angel – sparkly, light, magnificent."

Aliza lives in Bakersfield, working from her studio there when she's not on location in places like Los Angeles, New York, and Hong Kong.

She shared with us her inspiration, her philosophy, and her joy in offering her talents to the world:

"I'm so grateful for the opportunity to contribute to a more harmonious world. Humanity is enjoying renewed appreciation for the things we cherish, and more importantly the people we love. We want to create beauty and comfort in our lives. We want this world to be a brighter place to live in...and our inner lives are reflected in our homes and offices. That may be, simply, where a better world begins. It begins with us, and it begins where we live, (in) our interiors – both kinds. We all need beautiful objects in our lives, treasures that lift the heart and spirit during these uncertain times. We need art now, more than ever!"

Though she was referring specifically to her previous art book, *Pure Grace: Art & Inspiration*, her next words could apply to the sum of her art, and to the essence of who she is:

"It illustrates an affection for the childlike spirit and magical joy within us all. By awakening our creativity and compassion, it nourishes an understanding and appreciation for the magnificent world in which we live. I pray (it) will affirm the beauty of who we are and what we came here to do."

Aliza's two previous companion books, *The Dance of Love* and *Spirit of Joy* are currently available. Visit her web site at www.alizamccracken.com for more examples of her work and to learn more about this magnificent spirit.

Mary Lou Romagno
ECHOES Magazine

# Works of Art

*Thank you for helping to enrich the lives of others.  A portion of the proceeds will benefit the Make A Wish Foundation.*